TO. NORMAN (WHO I FOUND A VERY SINCERE PERSON)

FROM JIM. (O'NEILL)

The Parson's Quotation Book

The Parson's Quotation Book

A Literary Companion

THE REVEREND
GRAHAM JEFFERY

ROBERT HALE • LONDON

First published in Great Britain 1995

ISBN 0 7090 5300 2

Robert Hale Limited
Clerkenwell House
Clerkenwell Green
London EC1R 0HT

2 4 6 8 10 9 7 5 3 1

Printed and bound in Great Britain
by WBC Book Manufacturers Ltd.,
Bridgend, Mid Glamorgan.

Preface

When the Revd R. Taylor asked if he could be considered for a living in 1818 he received the curt reply, 'My dear Taylor. The background is the place for you.' As it is for every parson. A preacher is by definition one who enables other people to say wonderful things rather than saying them himself. The background however, while being a good place to serve, is not a good place to achieve fame or quotability. The better the priest, the less he is remembered or rather quoted. Which leaves the fame to some extent, to charlatans and attention seekers.

I have tried to redress this balance by quoting where possible unknown parsons, who have probably not been quoted before. I have tried also to keep this a parson's quotation book, rather than a vicar's one. For vicars are poor creatures, 'sloping' through the pages of Trollope. Smoothing with one hand their Brylcreemed hair, as we prepare to listen (Sassoon), and preaching always at us, never for us.

Parsons on the other hand are fat and friendly. Not 'vicarious' at all, they are the persons with the care of a particular place and people. They do not stand six foot above contradiction on Sunday, but belong to their people in their frailties and failures, as their people belong to them. They speak one day a week in the pulpit, and listen the other six. Mankind is their business (Dickens). Their church is co-extensive with humanity (Emil Mersch). And they are as religiously employed testing the owls' pitch in their garden (Gilbert White), as learning German on a storm-tossed ship in the Atlantic (John Wesley), the better to converse with fellow passengers.

It is true that the parson has failed in his calling. But that is the condition and danger of being human. He has turned 'Hoc est corpus' *into 'hocus pocus' at the altar of his God. More recently his parsonic voice has almost dwindled him into a vicar, and dwindled* 'Te Deum' *into tedium. But boring and tedious, his life never is. He, and now she, is the hidden thread of English history. And it is my devout wish and prayer that through the antics of this strange breed, Christianity may from time to time peep through.*

Graham Jeffery
Thakeham Rectory

Acknowledgements

Making acknowledgement for this collection has proved more difficult than the selection itself. The wind blows where it wants, and so do quotations. One hears the words, but no one knows where they have come from, or where they are going. Basil Hume's defining quotation of the priest's life for example, comes to me from the Revd W.G. Sinclair Snow's last sermon, at a scanty Evensong in St Wilfrid's Bognor Regis. I was entirely 'animated not dominated' by his moving words, thrown together I imagine by God's grace, hastily, as he prepared to hand over the key of his vestry to his churchwarden, and with only his wife and myself in attendance to say 'that's it, then'.

Many thanks to Bryan Cooper for his help in preparing the manuscript. Also to: the Revd Lord Soper; the Revd Dr Ian Paisley; the Revd Canon H.C.F. Copsey; Church Music Quarterly; *Lambeth Palace; Ewan MacNaughton Associates on behalf of the* Daily Telegraph *for the extract from the 'Peterborough' column; Mr Henry G. Button;* The Tablet; *HarperCollins Publishers Ltd for extracts from* Surprised by Joy, *by C.S. Lewis and* Chronicles of Wasted Time *by Malcolm Muggeridge; the Society of Authors on behalf of the Bernard Shaw Estate; BBC Enterprises Ltd for extracts produced from 'A Chip in the Sugar' from* Talking Heads *by*

Acknowledgments

Alan Bennett; John Johnson Ltd for extract from A Field Guide to the English Country Parson *published by William Heinemann Ltd, copyright © Thomas Hinde 1983; David Higham Associates Ltd for extract from* A Burnt Out Case *by Graham Greene published by Heinemann; SPCK for extract from* The Art of Preaching *by Charles Smyth (1940) and* The Country Parish Today and Tomorrow *by Frank West (1960); Mr Gerald Hill for his letter to the* Daily Telegraph; *Macmillan General Books for the use of 'The Country Clergy' by R.S. Thomas.*

Every effort has been made to contact all copyright holders but apologies are offered to those I may have overlooked and also to those whom I was unable to trace.

GRAHAM JEFFERY

Since there are no great preachers only great congregations, this book is offered not just to those who uttered but also to those who remembered the following words.

Christe's lore and his apostles twelve, he taught. But first he followed it himself.

GEOFFREY CHAUCER (*c.* 1343–1400)
The Canterbury Tales

The clergy of the Church of England are all that stand between this country and immediate religious revival.

GEORGE BERNARD SHAW (1856–1950)

I asked an inhabitant of a district close to Haworth what sort of clergyman they had at the church which he attended.

'A rare good one,' said he: 'he minds his own business, and ne'er troubles himself with ours.'

ELIZABETH GASKELL (1810–65)
The Life of Charlotte Brontë

Nice clergy who love their flock and look after them are as rare as hen's teeth, and need to be protected at all costs. Do look after yourself and take things very easy.

MARINA MIFSUD
March 1994

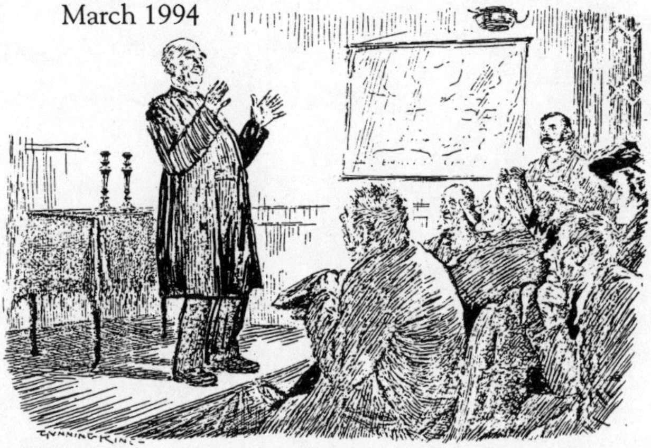

A priest should look upon himself as a physician of the soul.

DEAN W.R. INGE (1860–1954)

The priest's first duty is to survive.

GRAHAM GREENE (1904–91)
A Burnt out Case
1960

For anyone who has been a parish priest there can be no promotion. It is downhill all the way.

BISHOP PETER SSM
1989

It is not the priest's business to impose his own ideas, but to aid the workings of grace.

ABBÉ HUVELIN (1838–1910)

The clergy may be dreadful. But we have only the laity to choose from.

ANON

Clergy are men, as well as other folk.

HENRY FIELDING (1707–54)
Joseph Andrews

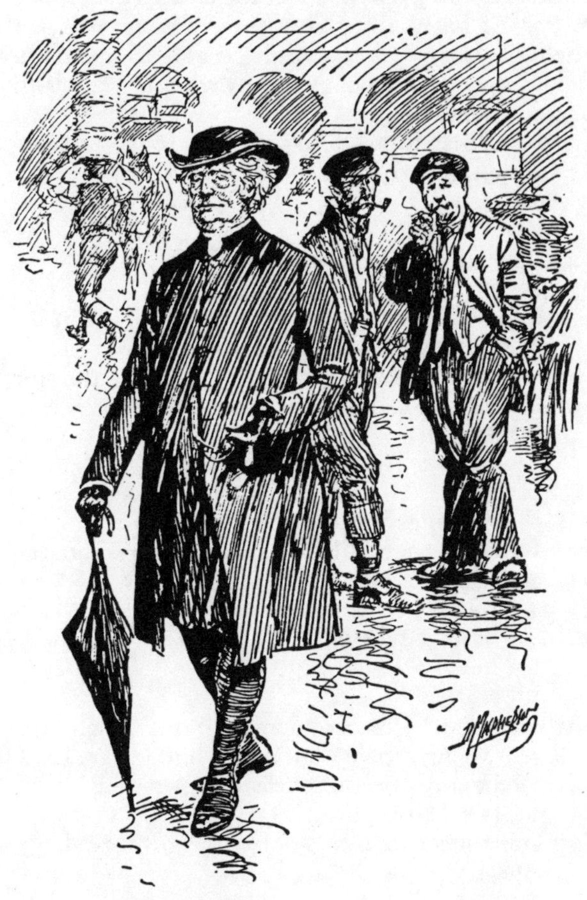

Sir, the life of a parson, of a conscientious clergyman, is not easy. I have always considered a clergyman as the father of a larger family than he is able to maintain. I would rather have Chancery suits upon my hands than the cure of souls.

SAMUEL JOHNSON (1709–84)
Boswell's *Life of Johnson*

I look upon all the world as my parish

JOHN WESLEY (1703–91)

What bishops like best in their clergy is a dropping-down-deadness of manner.

SYDNEY SMITH (1771–1845)
First Letter to Archdeacon Singleton

Then however, we still had a vague notion that clergymen believed in Christianity.

MALCOLM MUGGERIDGE
Chronicles of Wasted Time (1972)

Why I wondered did these unpretentious, delightful and intelligent young people want so much to live on £10,000 a year, and to carry on the battles of generations?

MICHAEL DE-LA-NOY
after a stay with some students at theological college

It will, I believe, be every where found, that as the clergy are, or are not what they ought to be, so are the rest of the nation.

JANE AUSTEN (1775–1817)
Mansfield Park

A very interesting man provided you can keep him off religion.

ANON
of Frederick W. Faber (1814–63)

A man that will hear you with patience, and relieve your necessities.

GEORGE HERBERT (1593–1633)
A Priest to the Temple

The clergyman is expected to be a kind of human Sunday.

SAMUEL BUTLER (1835–1902)
The Way of All Flesh

The priest's task is to animate not to dominate.

BASIL HUME (born 1923)

Ignorance in a priest is more harmful than sin.

ROMAN PROVERB

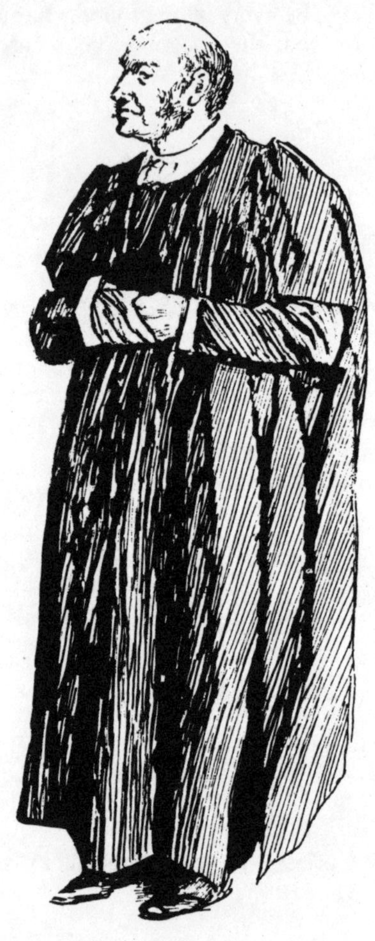

It's not enough to act as a priest, it's necessary to be one.

ANON

Invisible six days a week and incomprehensible on the seventh.

ANGLICAN PROVERB

There is nothing which exposes a priest more than to see him celebrate.

JACYNTH LAWRENCE
The Tablet, 12 June 1993

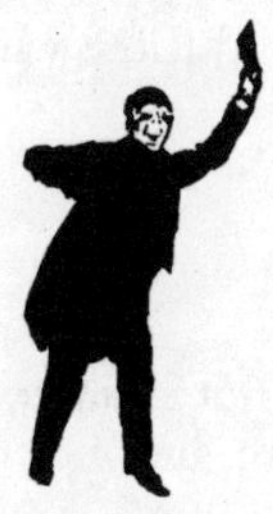

A clergyman cannot be high in state or fashion. He must not head mobs or set the tone in dress. But I cannot call that situation nothing, which has the charge of all that is of the first importance to mankind, individually or collectively considered, temporally and eternally – which has the guardianship of religion and morals and consequently of manners which result from their influence.

JANE AUSTEN (1775–1817)
Mansfield Park

I see them working in old rectories
by the sun's light, by candlelight,
Venerable men, their black cloth
A little dusty, a little green.
They left no books,
rather they wrote on men's hearts
and in the minds
Of young children sublime words
Too soon forgotten. God in his time
Or out of time will correct this.

R.S. THOMAS (1913–)

There are three sorts of country parson in my diocese. Those who have gone out of their minds. Those who are going of their minds. And those who have no minds to go out of.

ATTRIBUTED TO BISHOP EDWARD KING OF LINCOLN (1829–1910)

The inferior clergy are not numerous enough for their duties, as these duties are, beyond measure, minute and toilsome.

EDMUND BURKE (1729–97)
Reflections on the Revolution in France

The first year the new vicar can do no wrong. The second year he can do no right. The third year he is accepted as one who does well sometimes.

ANGLICAN PROVERB

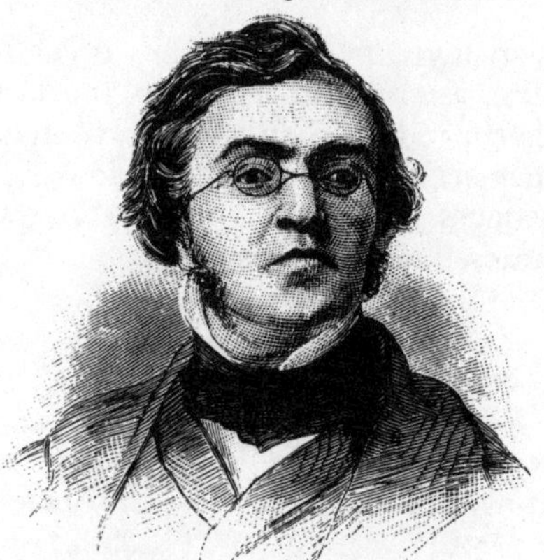

William Makepeace Thackeray

And I know this, that if there are some clerics who do wrong, there are straightaway a thousand newspapers to haul up those unfortunates, and cry 'Fie upon them. Fie upon them', while it somehow takes very little count of the many good ones.

W.M. THACKERAY (1811–63)

God gave us two ears and one mouth, so the Chinese proverb tells us. He seems however to have given most clergymen two mouths and no ear at all.

DONALD CARPENTER
Vicar of Hampden Park, Eastbourne
1962

Parsons are like manure. Spread about, they do a lot of good. But in a heap they stink.

ANON

Clergymen, in my experience, tend to get holier and holier looking, as they move farther and farther away from their faith; rather in the same way that a certain type of womaniser gets more ethereal looking the more women he seduces. It must be some kind of inner adjustment mechanics, like a thermostat.

MALCOLM MUGGERIDGE
Chronicles of Wasted Time, 1972

I dreamt last night I was in hell. It was just like this missionary meeting, I could not get near the fire for parsons.

BISHOP SAMUEL WILBERFORCE (1805–73)

Every bishop has a crook on his staff.

ANON

The see gives up its dead.

BISHOP IAN SHEVILL (1917–91)
attributed to a former bishop of London and quoted at the end of the North Queensland synod in 1964, in an attempt to secure young blood on the cathedral chapter – which appeal was promptly followed by the election of the elderly Wally Daniels (to tumultuous applause)

The bishop and Mr Harding loved each other warmly . . . I will not say they managed the diocese between them, but they spent much time in discussing the man who did.

ANTHONY TROLLOPE (1815–82)
The Warden

I have had a heaviness hang over me ever since I was nominated for this place.

ARCHBISHOP WILLIAM LAUD
Letter to Thomas Wentworth, 1633

The bishop knew how to entertain the clergy of his diocese, to talk easy small talk with the rectors' wives, and put curates at their ease; but it required the strong hand of the archdeacon to deal with such as were refractory either in their doctrines or their lives.

ANTHONY TROLLOPE (1815–82)
The Warden

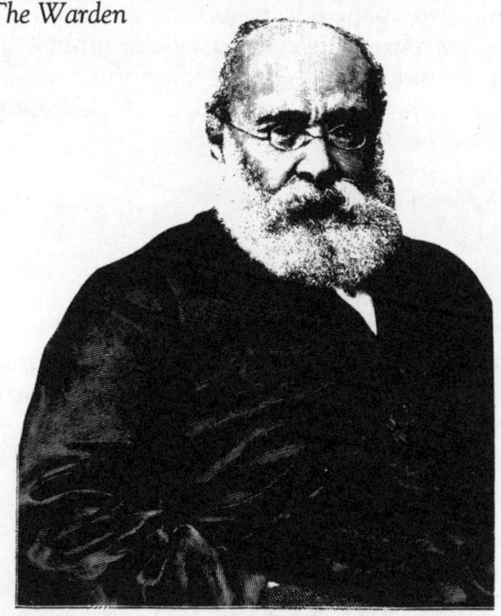

Anthony Trollope

I got ordained to do God a favour.

LORD SOPER

Lord, I will go wherever you want me to. But not India.

THE ACTS OF THOMAS
1st century AD

He had no oratorical graces. The matter of his sermons was dry, strained, dogmatic; the delivery harsh and unmusical. He could never learn to manage his voice. These defects were outweighted by the intense uncompromising earnestness of the preacher, his authoritative conviction of the supreme importance of his message.

GEOFFREY FABER
Oxford Apostles, 1945
on Edward Pusey

He confided rather pathetically to one of his old curates: 'You know, I have always felt that I should like to be a man to whom people would come instinctively with their troubles, but I find that I am not much more than a rather able administrator.'

CHARLES SMYTH
Cyril Forster Garbett, 1959

My dear Taylor, the background is the place for you.

BISHOP BUCKNER OF CHICHESTER
reply to the Revd Robert Taylor's request for a living, 1818

The wise lover thinks less of the gift than of the love which prompted it.

THOMAS À KEMPIS (c.1380–1471)
The Imitation of Christ

Earn all you can, save all you can, give all you can.

JOHN WESLEY (1703–91)
Journals

God always blesses a humble beginning, rather than those who start off with a chime of bells.

VINCENT DE PAUL (*c.* 1580–1660)

Christianity was not founded by clergymen.

NORMAN VINCENT PEALE
Faith for Today

In the evening I went very unwillingly to a society in Aldersgate Street, where one was reading Luther's preface to the Epistle to the Romans. About a quarter before nine . . . I felt my heart strangely warmed . . . I began to pray with all my might for those who had in a more especial manner despitefully used me and persecuted me.

JOHN WESLEY
24 May 1738
Journals

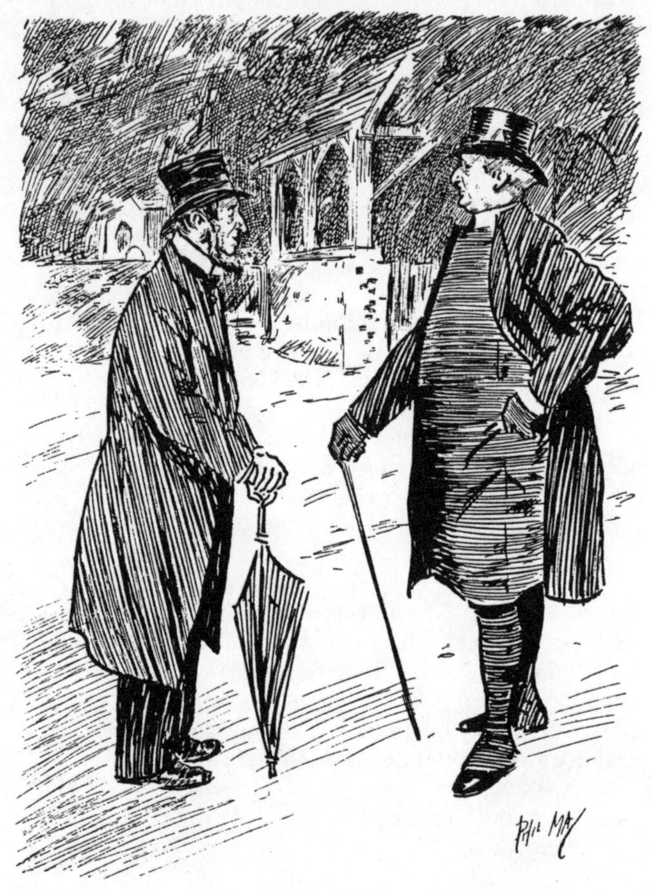
PHIL MAY

Every man has two journeys to make through life. The outer journey, with its various incidents and milestones . . . and the secret inner journey, of the soul.

DEAN W.R. INGE (1860–1954)

Upon this earth, a man cannot possibly make one step in a straight, and a direct line. The earth itself being round, every step we make upon it, must necessarily be a segment, an arch of a circle.

JOHN DONNE
5 November 1626

Man is curved in on himself.

MARTIN LUTHER (1483–1546)

Living in the country is nothing but a quiet grave.

SYDNEY SMITH (1771–1845)

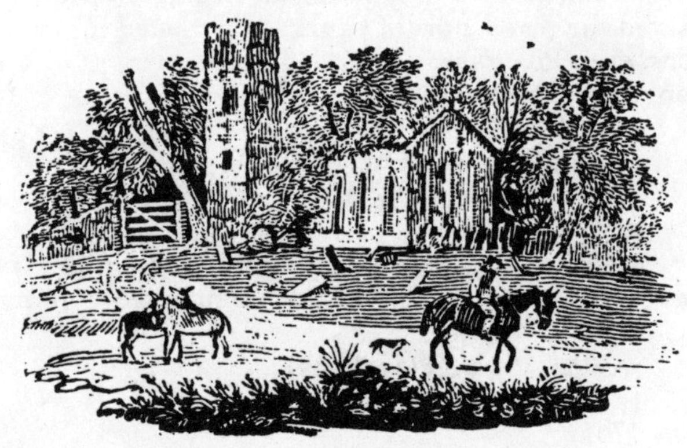

When the rector on his induction takes the key of the church, locks himself in, and tolls the bell, it is his own passing bell he is ringing. He is shutting himself out from any hope of a further career upon earth. He is a man transported for life . . . once a country parson, always a country parson.

AUGUSTUS JESSOPP
Rector of Scarning in Norfolk, 1895

Being a country parson is rather like playing fives against a haystack.

PROFESSOR NORMAN JUDD
Lecturer at Wells Theological College, 1958

The priest's heart is essentially maternal.

GERALD VANN OP (1906–63)

Neither do we read of any women in the Gospel, that assisted the persecutors of Christ, or furthered his afflictions; even Pilate's wife dissuaded it. Woman, as well as man, was made after the image of God.

JOHN DONNE
Sermon on Easter Day, 1630

A woman's preaching is like a dog walking on his hind legs. It is not done well, but you are surprised to find it done at all.

SAMUEL JOHNSON (1709–84)
Boswell's *London Journal*
1763

The idea that only a male can represent Christ at the altar is a most serious heresy.

BISHOP GEORGE CAREY
interview with David Moller, *Reader's Digest*, March 1991 in which he never doubts the integrity of those opposed to the ordination of women.

The Vicar of St Ives says the smell of fish there is sometimes so terrific as to stop the church clock.

FRANCIS KILVERT
21 July 1870

Too many clergymen have become keepers of an aquarium instead of fishers of men. And often they are just swiping each other's fish.

M.S. AUGSBURGER

It was once the proud boast of the Church of England that the parochial system ensured that there should be at least one educated gentleman resident in every parish of the kingdom. In every hamlet, however tiny and remote, there was a church, and next to the church a parsonage, and in the parsonage a parson . . . . When a detective in a Dorothy Sayers novel wanted to lay hands quickly on the complete works of Shakespeare, he went round to the local vicarage, expecting to find a parson in the study, and a Shakespeare on the bookshelves. He was not disappointed.

FRANK WEST (born 1909)
The County Parish Today and Tomorrow
1960

The Council (Vatican II) is like watching cricket. A wicket falls when you are not looking.

JOHN LAWRENCE
The Tablet, 12 June 1993

Another lady said that the dogs of Wootton Bassett were much more sociable than the people.

FRANCIS KILVERT
18 May 1870

My musical friend, at whose house I am now visiting, has tried all the owls that are his near neighbours with a pitch–pipe set at concert-pitch, and finds they all hoot in B flat. He will examine the nightingales next spring.
I am etc etc.

GILBERT WHITE
12 February 1771

NOV 22. I married Tom Burge of Ansford to Charity Andrews of C. Cary by License this morning. The Parish of Cary made him marry her, and he came handbolted to church for fear of running away, and the Parish of Cary was at all the expense of bringing of them.

JAMES WOODFORDE
The Diary of a Country Parson
1768

Friday, St Swithun's Day
Found Mrs Bevan sitting in the drawing room in full chat with Miss Wybrow. We had tea and then I went down to the Swan with Fanny and Nelly to fetch Miss Lynne and her brother to play croquet.

FRANCIS KILVERT
1870

Football is not a matter of life and death. It is far more important than that.

BILL SHANKLY
Quoted by Archbishop George Carey at his enthronement sermon on 19 April 1991

He must abstain some days from meat to clear his brain as also to let the blood, he should also take both purgatives and emetics to drive the humours from his body, and he must above all be sure to confess his sins and receive spiritual absolution just before sitting down to play in order to counteract the demoniacal influence of magic spells.

PIETRO CARRERA
creator of the Sicilian Defence, 1617

A Dorset clergyman has written a special collect as a prayer for English cricket. I did not altogether admire the collect itself, which has God bowling a googly, but the idea is not inappropriate.

WILLIAM REES-MOGG
The Times, 12 August 1993

An archbishop is entitled to six blackbirds at once.
A bishop is entitled to five blackbirds at once.
A dean is entitled to four blackbirds.
An archdeacon two.
If a dean has four dishes during his first course,
he is not allowed custard or fritters.

THOMAS CRANMER (1489–1556)
Archbishop Cranmer's Dietary
rations at an ecclesiastical luncheon

Heaven may be for the laity, but this world is certainly for the clergy.

GEORGE MOORE (1873–1958)

From reading the works of some modern writers of repute, you would fancy that a parson's life was passed in gorging himslf with plum-pudding and port wine.

W.M. THACKERAY (1811–63)

Most of us are preached out after six months. After six months we have said all we are going to say. From then on it is all repetition.

ARTHUR RYAN
Collinsville Parish Priest
North Queensland, 1965

That clergyman soon becomes an object of contempt who being often asked out to dinner never refuses to go.

JEROME (*c.* 342–420)

NOV. 17, MONDAY . . . Mr Maynard Rector of Morton called on me this Morning to ask my Advice, about one of his Parish by name Fisher, doing a kind of Penance next Sunday for calling Mrs. Michael Andrews, a Whore. He shewed me the form issued out of the Bishops Court. It is called a Deed of Retraction. A foolish kind of Affair between the parties, and the expences of which to both must be high. At 2. o'clock this Afternoon I walked to Weston Ch. and buried poor old Natl. Heavers, aged 85. Yrs. Dinner to day, a boiled Fowl & a Neck of Mutton rosted. My Ancle, thank God, continues finely. I still keep a thin Linnen Bandage upon it. Had a fat Pig killed this Morning by Tom Thurston, weight 8 Stone 4. lb.

JAMES WOODFORDE
The Diary of a Country Parson
1794

MAY 8, SUNDAY. By particular desire of Billy Gunton . . . himself with his Mistress Mrs. Michael Andrews, came to my House about 11. o'clock this Morning and I then had them into the Parlour and there administered the H. Sacrament to them and which I hope will be attended with due effects both to him, Mrs. Andrews & myself.

JAMES WOODFORDE
1796

Celibacy has kept Catholicism 'green' up till now . . . Protestantism has done much good, but one of its evils is that it has ridiculed celibacy.

MAHATMA GANDHI (1869–1948)

It is a great mistake to think God is only or chiefly concerned with religion.

ARCHBISHOP WILLIAM TEMPLE (1881–1944)

The young clergyman who asserted that he wasn't ordained to talk about pigs, showed himself to be very unsound in his theology.

FRANK WEST (born 1909)
The Country Parish Today and Tomorrow
1960

I do not want to do extraordinary things. I want to do ordinary things extraordinarily well.

THERESE OF LISIEUX (1873–97)
The Story of a Soul

He did a little thing well, while most of his contempories did big things badly.

OF THE REVD SAMUEL GRELLETT

A house-going parson makes a church-going people.

ANGLICAN PROVERB

Wyd was his parish, his houses far asunder

GEOFFREY CHAUCER (c. 1343–1400)
The Canterbury Tales

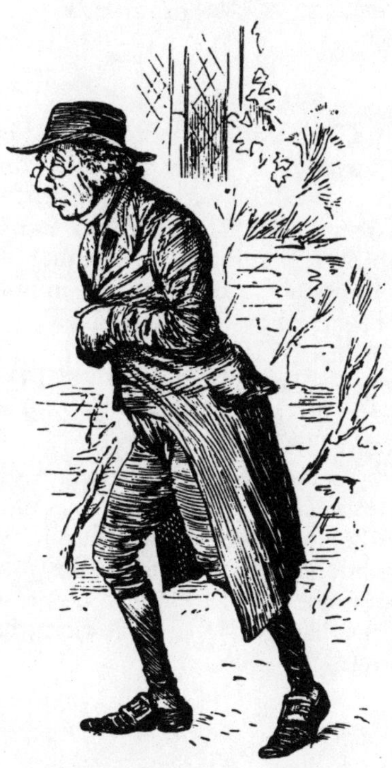

I am heartily weary of visiting so much as I have, but if did not it would be taken amiss in some.

JAMES WOODFORDE
The Diary of a Country Parson
11 January 1769

In a large parish you never see your parishioners, and in a small one you see nothing else.

BISHOP HENSLEY HENSON (1863–1947)

No ringing for Church in the morning, and but few people attended prayers; I heard the girls their catechism.

After church I walked with Joseph in the village to call upon a woman in Whitebrooks Lane . . . I am inclined to think it is actual laziness which keeps her in bed. The house smelt so bad that Joseph was obliged to leave it, and I soon followed his example.

JOHN SKINNER (1722–1839)
The Diary of a Somerset Rector 1803–1834. Being the parochial affairs of the parish of Camerton
25 March 1827
Rector of Camerton (1803–39). A dedicated priest and antiquarian, he ended his days estranged from his family and driven to suicide. Virginia Woolf wrote a brief account of his sad life, asking why no mercy was shown to him, and no respect, and no love? His diary asks these questions, but there are no answers.

In his own personal ministry the country parson lacks the stimulus which is given to the parish priest in the town. He must go at a slower pace, and the slower one goes the harder it is to keep moving at all.

FRANK WEST (born 1909)
The County Parish Today and Tomorrow
1960

I read Prayers and preached at Cary Church and whilst I was preaching one Thos Speed of Gallhampton came into the Church quite drunk and crazy and made a noise in the church, called the Singers a pack of Whoresbirds and gave me a nod or two in the pulpit. (The Constable Roger Coles Senr took him into custody after and will have him before a Magistrate to-morrow.)

JAMES WOODFORDE
The Diary of a Country Parson
15 July 1770

Friday 17. I began to learn German, in order to converse (a little)with the Moravians, six-and-twenty of whom we have on board, men who have left all for their Master, and who have indeed learned of Him, being meek and lowly, dead to the world, full of faith and of the Holy Ghost.

JOHN WESLEY
October 1735
Journals

Monday 20. In the afternoon Mr David Nitschmann, Bishop of the Moravians, Mr Van Hermdorf, and Andrew Dober, began to learn English.

JOHN WESLEY
October 1735

Easter Day. 17 April.

The happiest, brightest, most beautiful Easter I have ever spent. I woke early and looked out. As I had hoped the day was cloudless. a glorious morning. My first thought was 'Christ is Risen'. It is not well to lie in bed on Easter Morning, indeed it is thought very unlucky. I got up between five and six, and was out soon after six. There had been a frost, and the air was rimy . . . There were more communicants than usual: 29.

FRANCIS KILVERT
1870

July 1809

William Britain of Cridlingcot, died of a consumption, brought on in a great measure by excessive drinking. I attended him several times before his death, and he declared solemnly to me that the Red Post public house had been his ruin; that frequently on a Sunday he had left his home with the intention of going to Camerton Church, but as he crossed Whitebrooks Lane in his way thither something used to draw him away as it were, contrary to his better resolutions, and take him up the hill. He seemed to die very penitent.

JOHN SKINNER

The same month (March 1776) the Reverend Augustus Toplady, author of 'Rock of Ages', wrote an article in *Gospel* magazine in which he tried to explain that each human being commits 630,720,000 sins by the age of thirty.

ANDREW BARROW (born 1945)
The Flesh is Weak

All things work together for the good man, even his sins.

MEISTER ECKHART (c. 1260–1327)

You should think and deal with every man as a villain, without calling him so, or valuing him less.

DEAN JONATHAN SWIFT (1667–1745)

Patience is needed with everyone but first of all with ourselves

FRANCIS DE SALES (1567–1622)

I am delighted, Mr. Dean, that for once in your life you have condescended to allow Almighty God the happiness of giving you a little pleasure.

ELIZABETH GOUDGE
The Dean's Watch
1960

Of two evils, we should always choose the less.

THOMAS À KEMPIS (*c.* 1380–1671)

I regret the parson we sent to you has not proved acceptable, but having regard to the qualities you and your pcc require in your new rector, can only regret that the Archangel Gabriel is not available.

ANON
Archdeacon to churchwardens of a remote West Country parish
quoted by Prebendary Kenneth Haworth, *c.* 1959

OCT. 18 . . . I entirely forgot that this was St Luke's Day, and therefore did not read Prayers at C. Cary which I should have done otherwise. As it was not done willfully, I hope God will forgive it.

JAMES WOODFORDE
1766

MARCH 12. *Mem:* As I was going to shave myself this morning as usual on Sundays, my razor broke in my hand as I was setting it on the strop without any violence. May it be always a warning to me not to shave on the Lord's Day or do any other work to profane it pro futuro.

JAMES WOODFORDE
1769

Wherever we see the Word of God purely preached and heard, there a Church of God exists, even if it swarms with many faults.

JOHN CALVIN (1509–64)
Institutes of Religion

Evensong minus clergy is an excellent idea. Perhaps in the not too distant future, clergy will be dispensed with altogether, and choir and congregation can combine to provide an inspirational service.

CHURCH MUSIC QUARTERLY

He who cannot forgive others breaks the bridge over which he must pass himself.

GEORGE HERBERT (1593–1633)
A Priest to the Temple

MAY 22. . . . Have been very naughty to-day, did not go to either Ansford or Cary Church . . . Have mercy on me O Lord a miserable, vile sinner, and pardon my failings.

JAMES WOODFORDE
1774

NOV. 19. . . . Went this evening to Haw's [a famous Methodist] Lecture in St Giles Church . . . very stupid, low and bad stuff.

JAMES WOODFORDE
The Diary of a Country Parson
1761

Never be ashamed to own you have been in the wrong, tis but saying you are wiser today than you were yesterday.

DEAN JONATHAN SWIFT (1667–1745)

Do not try to break difficulties and contradictions, bend them with gentleness and time.

FRANCIS DE SALES (1567–1622)

Sin boldly.

MARTIN LUTHER (1483–1546)

The business of finding fault is very easy: that of doing better, very difficult.

FRANCIS DE SALES (1567–1622)

The habit of hearing confessions seemed to have a bad effect on Dr. Pusey. The curiosity which he tried to repress in the ordinary affairs of life broke out in an almost morbid interest in the spiritual ailments of others. He would cross-question all manner of people about the state of their souls, their inmost wishes, habits, intentions.

MARK PATTISON
1843

Sunday 15 May 1763
. . . went to Dr. Fordyce's meeting in Monkwell Street and heard Dr. Blair preach. I thought this would have done me good. But I found the reverse. Blair's New Kirk delivery and the Dissenters roaring out the Psalms sitting on their backsides, together with the extempore prayers, and in short the whole vulgar idea of Presbyterian worship, made me very gloomy. I therefore hastened from this place to St. Paul's, where I heard the conclusion of service, and had my mind set right again.

JAMES BOSWELL
London Journal

Christianity has taught us to care. Caring is the greatest thing.

BARON VON HÜGEL (1852–1925)

Kindness gives birth to kindness.

SOPHOCLES (496–406 BC)

Christianity is caught not taught.
DEAN W.R. INGE (1860–1954)

But though I liked clergymen as I liked bears, I had as little wish to be in the Church as in the zoo . . . To me, religion ought to have been a matter of good men praying alone and meeting by twos and threes to talk of spiritual matters. And then the fussy, time wasting botheration of it all! The bells, the crowds, the umbrellas, the notices, the perpetual arranging and organising. Hymns were (and are) extremely disagreeable to me. Of all musical instruments I liked (and like) the organ least. I have, too, a sort of spiritual gaucherie which makes me unapt to participate in any rite.
C.S. LEWIS (1898–1963)
Surprised by Joy, 1955

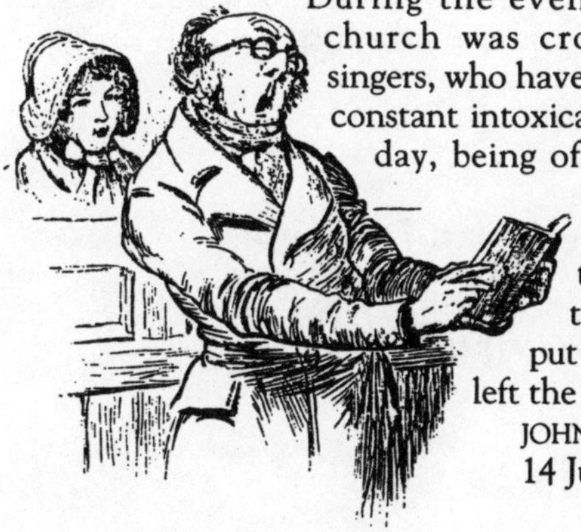

During the evening service the church was crowded; and the singers, who have been in a state of constant intoxication since yesterday, being offended because I would not suffer them to chant the service after the First Lesson, put on their hats and left the Church.
JOHN SKINNER
14 July 1822

On my speaking to her very seriously on her notorious neglect of all religious and moral duties and the danger of putting of repentance to the last, she said if God would permit her to live only a few months longer she would be quite a new creature, she would not swear, nor drink again, indeed she would sell her coal horse and not drive coal again to Bath, for that was the way she got into liquor stopping at public houses by the wayside and falling into evil company.

The woman contrary to expectation, got about again; but instead of selling her coal horse and abstaining from drink etc. she got worse than ever and indeed threatened to kill her husband with a knife.

JOHN SKINNER
1811

I am always very well pleased with a country Sunday; and think if keeping holy the seventh day were only a human institution, it would be the best method that could have been thought of for the polishing and civilizing of mankind.

JOSEPH ADDISON (1672–1719)

Sunday. To Trinity Church, Dorchester.
The rector delivers himself of mean images in a sublime voice.

THOMAS HARDY (1840–1928)

Grace not Grease.

IAN PAISLEY
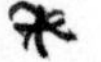
Sermon in Martyrs Memorial Church, Belfast, 1975

A parson should light fires in a dark room, and go on lighting them all his life.

DICK SHEPPARD (1880–1937)
wartime vicar of St Martin in the Fields, London. He once stopped a zealous churchwarden from waking an exhausted serviceman during the sermon. The following day the papers read 'Vicar supports Sleeping in Church'.

This merriment of parsons is mighty offensive.

SAMUEL JOHNSON (1709–84)

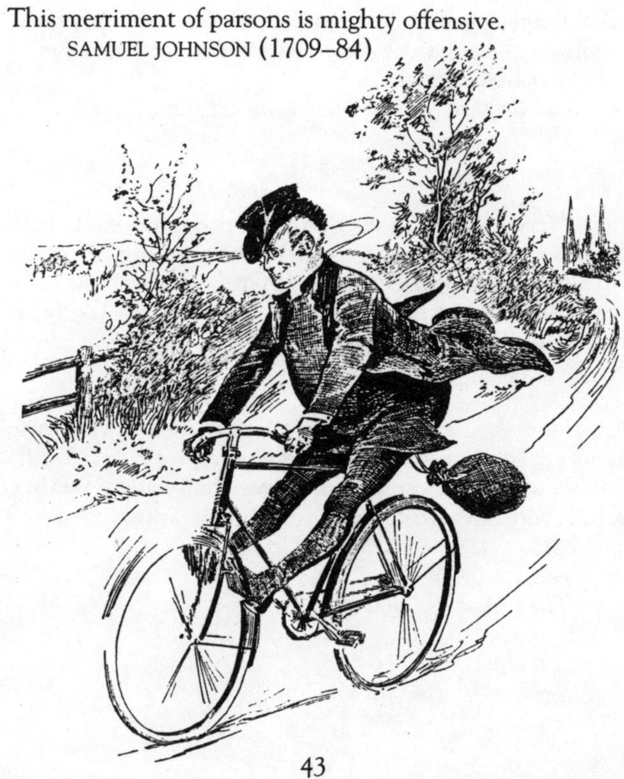

Preach the Gospel to every creature. Use words if necessary.

FRANCIS OF ASSISI (1181/2–1226)

Judge not the preacher, he judges you.

GEORGE HERBERT (1593–1633)
A Priest to the Temple

I don't agree that there are no great preachers only great congregations. But the congregation needs to be hungry.

CHARLES SAYERS
Lay preacher in the Harrogate circuit
1994

Never forget. The more trouble the sermon is for you, the less it is, in general, for your congregation.

PREBENDARY KENNETH HAWORTH
in conversation at Wells Theological College, where he was Principal (*c*. 1958)

A sermon should be like a love letter. Before you write it, you do not know what you are going to write. While you are writing it, you do not know what you are writing. When you have written it, you do not know what you have said.

PROFESSOR DALE
The Preacher's Notebook

First I tells 'em what I'm going to say, then I tells 'em. Then I tells them what I've said.

BAPTIST PREACHER

Read yourself full, pray yourself hot, let them have it.

ANON

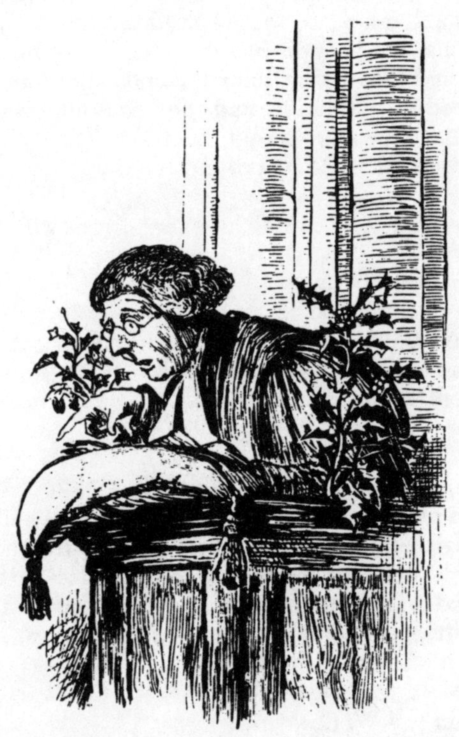

The bell that rings to a sermon calls not upon the preacher only, but upon the congregation to come, so this bell calls us all.

JOHN DONNE (1572–1631)

Oh, my dear, when you have a clergyman in your family you must accommodate your tastes: I did that very early. When I married Humphrey I made up my mind to like sermons, and I set out by liking the end very much. That soon spread to the middle and the beginning, because I couldn't have the end without them.

GEORGE ELIOT (1819–80)
Middlemarch
speech by Mrs Cadwallader, the rector's wife

A priest is one who draws back the curtain that separates man from God and is lost in the folds.

ANON

Pusey is returned . . . and in appearance much better. It is no exaggeration to say he is a Father in the face and aspect. He has been preaching to breathless congregations at Exeter and Brighton. Ladies have been sitting on the pulpit steps, and sentimental paragraphs have appeared in the papers.

JOHN HENRY NEWMAN (1801–90)
Letter to J.W. Bowden

Unlike his fellow evangelists, Father Ignatius never succumbed to the temptation to mingle the pure milk of the Gospel with denunciation of current abuses.

PETER HAMMOND
The Waters of Marah
1956

The worst of Warburton is, he has a rage for saying something when there is nothing to be said.

SAMUEL JOHNSON (1709–84)
to Mr Burney c. 1758, the year before William Warburton became Bishop of Gloucester.
Life of Johnson

He who preaches twice, prates once.

ANON

The preacher's job is to feed the sheep, not entertain the goats.

PREBENDARY KENNETH HAWORTH

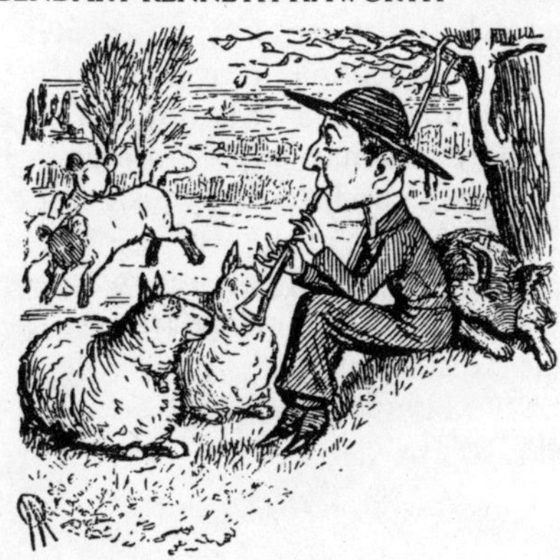

Sir, it is owing to their expressing themselves in a plain and familiar manner . . . the only way to do good to the common people.

SAMUEL JOHNSON (1709–84)
Boswell's *London Journal*, 1763
on the success of the Methodist preachers

The only persons truly anxious to hear the Preacher were a few antiquated devotees, and half a dozen rival Orators, determined to find fault with and ridicule the discourse. As to the remainder of the Audience, the Sermon might have been omitted altogether, certainly without their being disappointed, and very probably without their perceiving the omission.

MATTHEW LEWIS
The Monk
1769

We do not look in great cities for our best morality. It is not there, that respectable people of any denomination can do most good; and it certainly is not there, that the influence of the clergy can be most felt. A fine preacher is followed and admired; but it is not in fine preaching only that a good clergyman will be useful in his parish and his neighbourhood, where the parish and neighbourhood are of a size capable of knowing his private character, and observing his general conduct, which in London can rarely be the case. The clergy are lost there in the crowds of their parishioners.

JANE AUSTEN (1775–1817)
Mansfield Park

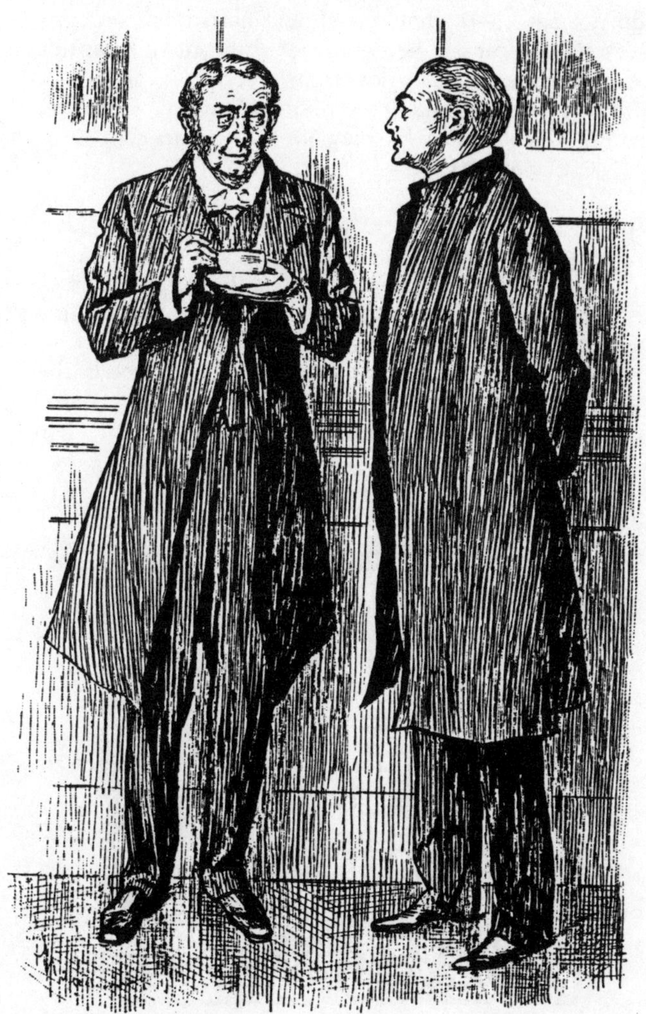

I do not agree, sir, that one should burn one's sermons every seven years: it being a poor thing, if one cannot preach a better sermon now than seven years ago. Not so. For if God has blessed a sermon twenty-five years ago, there is no reason why He may not do so again.

JOHN WESLEY (1703–91)

William Haslam, nineteenth-century minister of Baldhu in Cornwall, was converted by his own sermon. Preaching initially on the text 'What think ye of Christ?' he 'became aware of a wonderful light and joy' coming into him, and 'began to see what the Pharisees did not.'

Suddenly a local preacher, who happened to be in the congregation stood up and putting up his arms, shouted in the Cornish manner, 'The parson is converted. The parson is converted. Hallelujah.'

DAVID HAY
Review in *The Tablet*, 18 September 1993

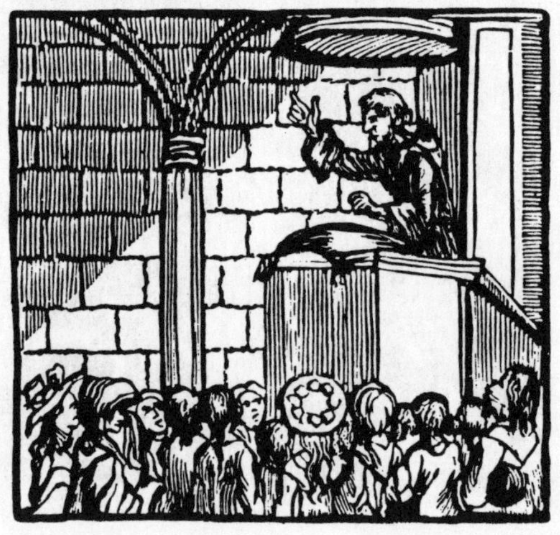

At first not many heard, the noise around us being exceeding great. But the silence spread farther and farther, till I had a quiet attentive congregation.

JOHN WESLEY
Journal
14 September 1740

(I then read) Ogden's second and ninth sermons on prayer, which, with their other distinguished excellence, have the merit of being short.

JAMES BOSWELL (1740–95)
London Journal

The Christian Church is the one organisation in the world that exists purely for the benefit of non-members.

ARCHBISHOP WILLIAM TEMPLE (1881–1944)

The church which is married to the Spirit of its Age will be a widow in the next.

DEAN W.R. INGE (1860–1954)

There is little good in filling churches with people who go out exactly as they came in; the call of the Church is not to fill churches but to fill heaven.

ANDREW SDC
The Way of Victory
founder of the Society of the Divine Compassion

The Church is the only institution in the world that has lower entrance requirements than those for getting on a bus.

WILLIAM LAROE

Churches in cities are most wonderful solitudes.

THOMAS MERTON
The Sign of Jonas

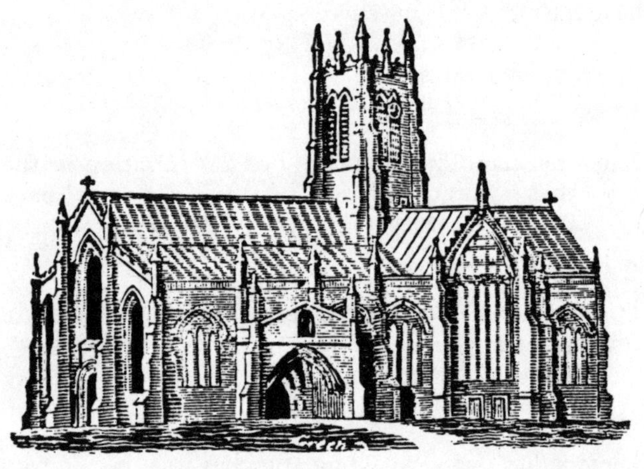

The only trouble with the barbarian nations being converted to Christianity was that they made more difference to the church than the church did to the barbarians.

BISHOP CHARLES GORE (1853–1932)

We live in an Age that hath more need of good examples than precepts.

GEORGE HERBERT (1593–1633)
A Priest to the Temple

The word of God . . . is a kind of river, both shallow and deep, where the lamb may find a footing and the elephant float.

POPE GREGORY I (*c.* 540–604)

A writer is in some sort a preacher: though his tongue be silent, his pen preaches, and a sermon preached from the Press sometimes edifies so much the more than from the pulpit.

HENRY KING (1592–1669)
Bishop of Chichester

My dear child, you must believe in God in spite of what the clergy may tell you.

BENJAMIN JOWETT
quoted in the conclusion of Neville Cardus's Autobiography, 1942

Ten thousand difficulties do not make one doubt.

JOHN HENRY NEWMAN (1801–90)

When unhappy, one doubts everything; when happy, nothing.

JOSEPH ROUX

No, I had not heard the new theology that God was dead. I didn't even know that He was ill.

LORD SOPER

I experienced a glorious sense of freedom when I plucked up the courage to say, I do not believe in God.

ANTHONY FREEMAN (born 1946)
the Rector of Staplefield who was obliged to leave his parish in 1994 because of his theological beliefs

I asked a Roman Catholic padre at the front once, what he would do if it was proved to him that there was no God. He replied that it would make no difference to his work at all. He would continue comforting the sick and bereaved, and giving the dying the assurance that there was one who loved them and that their living had not been in vain.

DONALD HANKEY
A Student in Arms
1916

I preached in the morning at Camerton a sermon, pointing out the advantages of education if properly directed, and the ills arising from the neglect of it. Mrs Jarrett, I thought, did not seem much to approve of some parts of the discourse, as I now and then noticed an emphatic 'hem'. However, I am too old a soldier to be alarmed at squibs!

JOHN SKINNER
10 August 1823

No mention of God. They keep him up their sleeve for as long as they can, vicars do. They know it puts people off.

ALAN BENNETT (1934–)
Talking Heads

The Gospel was not good advice but good news.

DEAN W.R. INGE (1860–1954)

Mr Gilfil's sermons . . . were not of a highly doctrinal, still less a polemical cast amounting indeed to little more than . . those who do wrong will find it the worse for them, and those who do well will find it the better.

GEORGE ELIOT (1819–80)
Scenes of Clerical Life

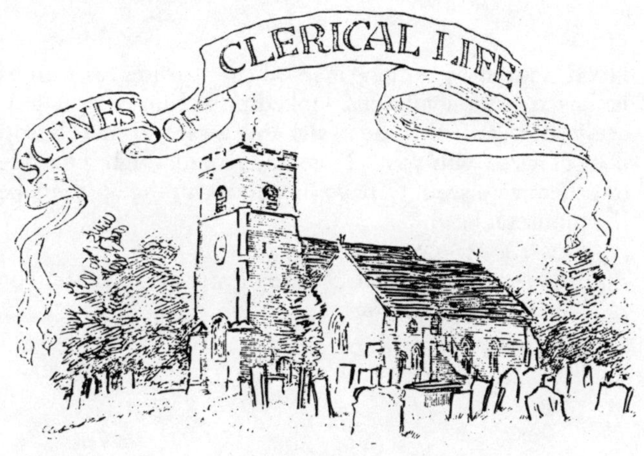

There is perhaps no greater hardship at present inflicted on mankind in civilised and free countries than the necessity of listening to sermons. No one but a preaching clergyman has in these realms the power of compelling an audience to sit silent and be tormented. No one but a preaching clergyman can revel in platitudes, truisms and un-truisms and yet receive as his undisputed privilege the same respectful demeanour as though words of impassioned eloquence or persuasive logic fell from his lips. A member of parliament can be coughed down or counted out, town councillors can be tabooed, but no one can rid himself of the preaching clergyman. He is the bore of the age, the nightmare that disturbs our Sunday's rest, the incubus that overloads our religion and makes God's service distasteful.

ANTHONY TROLLOPE (1815–82)
Barchester Towers

Hood, visited by a clergyman whose features, as well as language, were lugubrious, looked up at him compassionately and said, 'My dear sir, I'm afraid your religion doesn't agree with you.' The same remark might be made to others who seem to have just enough religion to make them miserable.

C.H. SPURGEON (1834–92)
Salt-cellars; A collection of Proverbs together with homely notes thereon

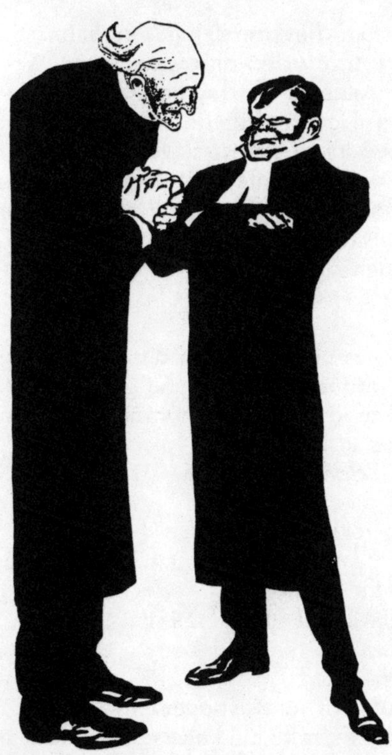

I could scarce reconcile myself at first to 'this strange way of preaching in the fields' . . . having been all my life (till very lately) so tenacious of every point relating to decency and order, that I should have thought the saving of souls almost a sin, if it had not been done in a church.'

JOHN WESLEY
29 March 1739
Journal

I have a dream that one day this nation will rise up and live out the true meaning of its creed: 'We hold these truths to be self evident: that all men are created equal.'

I have a dream, that one day on the red hills of Georgia the sons of former slaves and the sons of former slave-owners will be able to sit down together at the table of brotherhood.

MARTIN LUTHER KING
28 August 1963

An inscription over a church door in Cheshire: 'This is the House of God. This is the gate of heaven. (This door is locked in the winter months)'

PETERBOROUGH
Daily Telegraph

He cannot have God for his father who refuses to have the church for his mother.

AUGUSTINE OF HIPPO (354–430)

The great door sighs. It opens and a child
Enters the Church and kneels in the front pew.
The maker of the Universe has smiled:
He made the Church for this one interview.

DANIEL SARGENT
God's Ambuscade: 'The Village Church'

Full of dead men's bones, and potential love.

LIONEL JOHNSON

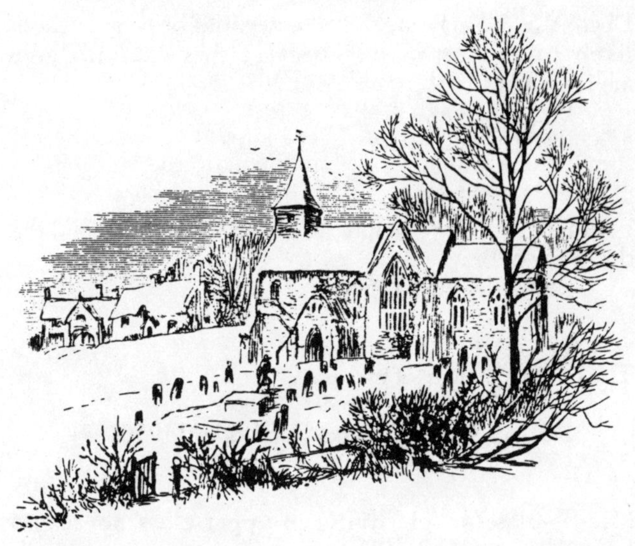

Quite cold and dead, fitter for sleep than prayer.

JOHN WESLEY
27 October 1739
Journals

The church can recover from unchaste priests, drunk priests, priests who have lost their faith. But never from unkind priests.

MANUAL OF CATHOLIC INSTRUCTION
c. 1961

Doctors and clergy are, of all categories of people, those likely to be most useless, because they can only give advice, and cannot listen.

DR FRANK LAKE
medical missionary

I always keep my principle, which is this, to live and die the Vicar of Bray.

SAMUEL ALEYNE (1540–88)

The endless chatter of parsons.

ALEC VIDLER (born 1899)
Dean of King's College, Cambridge (1956–67)

Middle-class people living in upper-class houses on lower-class incomes.

ANON

Miss Austen, 16 Nov. 1815
No 23 Hans Place,
Sloane Street.

. . . And I also dear Madam wished to be allowed to ask you, to delineate in some future Work the Habits of Life and Character and enthusiasm of a Clergyman – who should pass his time between the metropolis & the Country – who should be something like Beatties Minstrel

Silent when glad, affectionate tho' shy
And now his look was most demurely sad

& now he laughd aloud yet none knew why –

Neither Goldsmith – nor La Fontaine in his Tableau de Famille – have in my mind quite delineated an English Clergyman, at least of the present day – Fond of, & entirely engaged in Literature – no man's Enemy but his own. Pray dear Madam think of these things.

Believe me at all times
With sincerity & respect
Your faithful & obliged Servant
J.S. Clarke
Librarian.

J.S. CLARKE
from *Jane Austen's Letters to her Sister Cassandra and Others*. ed. R.W. Chapman (OUP, 1932)

The trouble with the Church of England is that all the people are in the towns and all the clergy are in the country.

ANON

If anything, it is far more difficult to be a country parson than a town one. In London I used to have sixteen people of a Sunday, to carry me in. Here one is face to face with people. One cannot escape their needs. And of course it is far more difficult to preach to a small congregation, than to a large one.

FREDDIE KERR DINEEN
Archdeacon of Chichester
c. 1974

A man who talks once a week, and it takes two people to carry up the money.

ANON

If the clergy are not taught how to preach, it is equally true that barristers are not taught how to plead, and dons are certainly not taught how to lecture.

CHARLES SMYTH
The Art of Preaching, 1940

I am, quite honoured by your thinking me capable of drawing such a clergyman. But I assure you I am not. The comic part of the character I might be equal to, but not the good, the enthusiastic, the literary.

A classical education, or at any rate a very extensive education with English literature, appears to be quite indispensable for the person who would do any justice to your clergyman.

JANE AUSTEN (1775–1817)
letter to James Stanier Clarke, 1815

For a priest ought not only to be pure, as being honoured with a great ministry. He should also be very intelligent, and experienced in many affairs, and even equally skilful in all secular business, with those who are engaged in it, while he must yet be more entirely detached from the love of it than anchorites who resort to the mountains.

BISHOP JOHN CHRYSOSTOM (*c.* 347–407)

I had rather ye should come of a naughty mind, to hear the word of god, for novelty . . . than to be away. I should rather ye should come . . . as the Gentelwoman of London . . . Marry, said she, I am going to St Thomas of Acres to the sermon, I could not sleep al this last night, and I am going now thither, I never failed of a good nap there.

And so, I had rather ye should go a napping to the sermons, than not to go at al.

BISHOP HUGH LATIMER
sermon before King Edward VI, 12 April 1549

The main burden of Mr —'s sermon was that it was good to be good, but bad to be bad, which while being true and unexceptionable, I had previously gathered from other sources.

BERNARD TANNER
1970

I preached to a crowded audience, so great indeed, the church could not contain them. They were for the most part attentive to the discourse, which spoke of Death and Immortality. I must say, I was not a little hurt at the total want of all propriety in the people after the service was concluded, since instead of returning quietly to their respective homes in order to reflect on the subject I had taken so much pains to impress on their minds, and which had so fully occupied my own, they banish at once all serious reflection by a merry peal.

JOHN SKINNER
29 July 1821

He was not only the best preacher of his day, but seemed to have brought preaching to perfection. His sermons were so well heard and liked, and so much read, that all the Nation proposed him as a pattern and studied to copy after him.

BISHOP GILBERT BURNETT on John Tillotson, 1734
History of My Own Time

As soon as the sermon is finished, nobody presumes to stir till Sir Roger is gone out of the church. The knight walks down from his seat in the chancel between a double row of his tenants, that stand bowing to him on each side; and every now and then he enquires how such an one's wife, or mother, or son, or father do, whom he does not see at church; which is understood as a secret reprimand to the person that is absent.

JOSEPH ADDISON (1672–1719)
The Spectator, no. 112

The nice conceited Word of Man is not to be substituted for the plain and saving Word of Christ.

QUOTED BY BISHOP HENSLEY HENSON (1863–1947)

Found I could with great ease make allusion to passages connected with the subject . . . I feel convinced that with a little practice, I could express myself without any kind of hesitation; not that I ever mean to adopt extemporaneous preaching.

JOHN SKINNER
1824

The Revd Frederick Cavell, father of Edith, took literally the saying of St. Paul, that we should preach without ceasing, in season and out of season. He preached the same sermon to his country congregation every Sunday word for word, for 48 years.

Chichester Diocesan News

Sermons to order

Sir – It would seem that many people are discouraged from going to church by the prospect of having to sit through the kind of sermons discussed by the Rev. Ian Gregory (letter, Feb 12), who proposes a good preacher guide.

My grandfather had a foolproof way of dealing with the problem. It was his custom to sit in the front row at church, and at the beginning of the sermon he would lay out his proposed contribution to the day's collection, in full view of the pulpit.

When he considered that the parson had said enough, at 60-second intervals he would very pointedly flip one coin at a time off the pew back into his purse. Seeing the law of diminishing returns 'raw in tooth and claw', the parson rapidly learnt to draw to a conclusion.

GERALD HILL
Daily Telegraph, 1994

If all you are going to say is a few words, then the fewer the better.

CANON JOHN JONES
lecturer at Wells Theological College
1958

Why do Presbyterian ministers talk more than other men? They don't: it only seems that they do.

GEORGE MACLEOD
founder of the Iona Community

Being preached to by that [Baptist Minister] was like being steamed like a potato.

CHARLES DICKENS (1812–70)

I'm no standin' here to bless a plateful of thruppences.

SCOTTISH PARSON
quoted by Prebendary Kenneth Haworth

During the Rev. Morgan Jones' whole forty-three years at Blewbury (1781–1824) he wore the same coat and hat. When the black hat collapsed he replaced its brim with a brown one from a scarecrow. His coat was so patched and darned that it was reduced to the size of a jacket. For many years after he died a parishioner preserved it in a glass case . . . he wrote a thousand sermons but never had them printed because he would not risk the postage to offer them to a publisher.

THOMAS HINDE
A Field Guide to the English Country Parson
1983

This gave me an opportunity of witnessing also the benevolence of a brother clergyman (Glossop of Wolverton), which rose him highly in my estimation. A poor blind man, who had been led in by the chancel door during the service, felt his way up to the seat before which Glossop was kneeling and placed himself in it. Glossop immediately rose from his knees, went to the back of a pew beyond, where he stood till the sermon was concluded, leaving his seat to be enjoyed by the poor blind man.

At dinner I endeavoured to imitate this truly clerical conduct of the worthy rector.

JOHN SKINNER

He is a first rate clergyman, able to say what he likes to whom he likes, to lecture people without setting up himself against them, to impose his authority on them without humiliating them, and, on occasion, to interfere in their business without impertinence!

GEORGE BERNARD SHAW (1856–1950)
description of the Revd James Mavor Morell in *Candida*

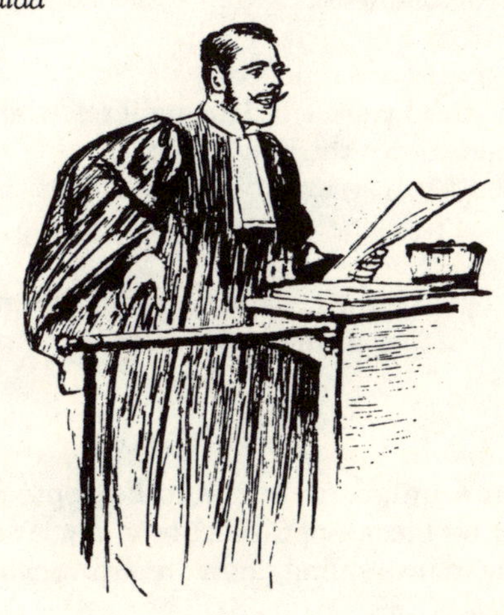

If you have not struck oil after ten minutes, stop boring.
ANON

I was up early, and commenced writing the sermon I have for some time been reflecting on, respecting the awful departure of Charles Dando, on the text 'Let us eat and drink for tomorrow we die'. I had ever made a point during the whole of my Ministry, not to be personal in my sermons, and therefore should not mention any names or particulars, but I conceived it my duty not to let slip this solemn opportunity of impressing the necessity of reformation, lest we be cut off suddenly, and it be too late.
JOHN SKINNER
1821

A sermon is seldom as long as it seems.
SAMUAL CROTHERS

A fine sermon did you say? The devil said the very same to me as I came down the pulpit steps.
ATTRIBUTED TO DWIGHT LYMAN MOODY (1837–99)

t If all the people who went to sleep during sermons were laid end to end, they would be far more comfortable.
ANON

Preaching is a unique privilege to be approached with godly fear. To break open the lively oracles of God, to proclaim the transforming and converting word of Jesus

Christ, is no casual duty, to be served by a fit of fevered activity last thing on a Saturday night; or worse still, to be spoken of in disparaging terms by the very people who have been called and ordained to that ministry.

To refer to one's preaching as 'what the congregation has to suffer', or to make promises that 'this won't be long', does nothing to raise the expectations that preaching might be a time of significance or revelation.

CHURCH OF SCOTLAND PANEL ON WORSHIP

Telling jokes and preaching sermons are two activities that are much more difficult than they seem at first.

A man who can do both at the same time is very rare indeed.

MARGARET HOWARD
The Tablet, 30 October 1993

Sir, Some earlier generations would have regarded a sermon lasting only 45 minutes as pretty short measure. One man who evidently had mastered the art of holding the attention of his congregation for longer than that was Laurence Chaderton, a former Fellow of Christ's College, who became in 1584, the first Master of Emmanuel College and lived to be 102.

On one occasion, when he had been preaching for two hours, he is said to have shown signs of flagging. The congregation then cried out, with one voice: 'For God's sake, Sir, go on!'

HENRY BUTTON
letter to *The Times*, 12 April 1994

I preached in the evening at Wednesbury, where, notwithstanding the rain, every man, woman and child stayed to the end.

JOHN WESLEY
3 April 1751
Journal

I read prayers in the morning to a thin congregation.

JOHN SKINNER
10 February 1828

It seems to me that the absurdity, as it appears to many, of Tom Keble's daily plan is, his praying to empty benches. Put yourself near the altar and you may be solitary.

JOHN HENRY NEWMAN (1801–90)
on the Revd Thomas Keble's reintroduction of daily Matins and Evensong in church, as directed in the Prayer Book

The fewer the words the better the prayer.

MARTIN LUTHER (1483–1546)

If I have fifty letters waiting to be answered, as is the case for a busy bishop, then I answer the first five and commend the rest to God.

FRANCIS DE SALES (1567–1622)

Hatch, match and dispatch.

ANGLICAN PROVERB

Most of your parishioners will only meet you on three occasions. The first and last, baptism and burial, they are not conscious at all. And the middle one, holy matrimony, they are barely half conscious, if that.

PREBENDARY KENNETH HAWORTH

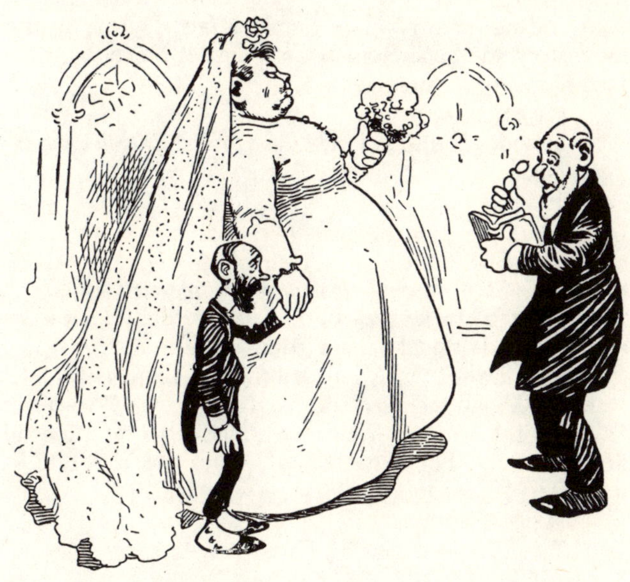

Do you promise to love, honour and – er – obey this man?

Taken as a whole, country parsons suggest some sociological experiment: give a reasonably educated middle-class Englishman a modest income, a house in the country, and job security for life, and see what he will do. He does remarkable things. He becomes a world authority on spiders . . . he plants 5,000 rose bushes in his garden and the surrounding countryside . . . makes his Rectory into a monastery and turns Roman Catholic . . . breeds winning race-horses or green mice.

THOMAS HINDE
introduction to *A Field Guide to The English Country Parson*
1983

MAY 29. At nine o'clock this morning went to Christ Church with Hooke, and Pitters, to be ordained Deacon; and was ordained Deacon there by Hume Bishop of Oxford. There were 25 Ordained Deacons and 13 Priests. We all received the Sacrament . . . We were in C. Church Cathedral from nine o'clock this morning till after twelve. For wine this afternoon in the B.C.R. pd. 0.0.6

JAMES WOODFORDE
The Diary of a Country Parson
1763

I had had occasion to notice the behaviour of a woman of the name of Sarah Summers, who kept company with Coward, a servant of Burfitt's.

In the beginning of November, 1806, she came to me saying she wished to have the Banns asked between Coward and herself. I told her that it had been mentioned to me that her husband was alive, and therefore it would be very wrong in her to think of being asked without she was certain he was dead. She said it was all false what folks said about him being alive; that he went to the East Indies as soldier upwards of seven years ago, and had never been heard of since.

I accordingly asked the Banns in Church. Just as the parties were preparing to be married the husband made his appearance at Camerton, and on enquiring for his wife found out her residence and surprised her by his coming so unexpectedly upon her; whilst he on his part was no less astonished at finding four children, instead of the one he had left when he went abroad.

JOHN SKINNER
January 1807

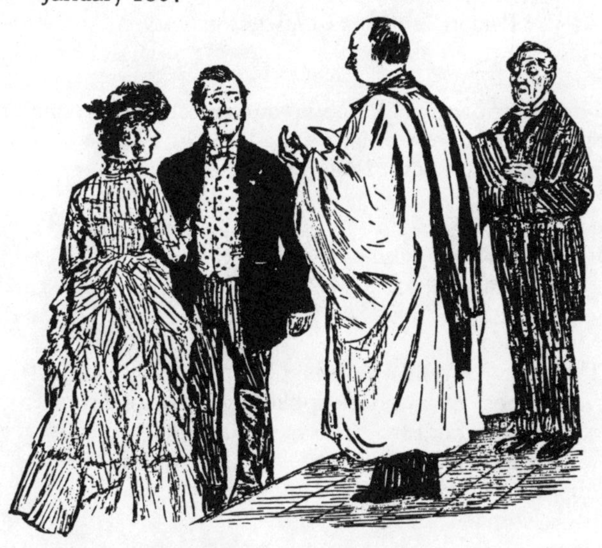

As soon as the bells began to ring I went to the Church to request we might have no more rejoicing, as we had been surfeited with it the last week

JOHN SKINNER
14 July 1822

It is possible to be both a Tory and a Christian. But only a bad Christian.

BISHOP TREVOR HUDDLESTON (born 1913)

A parson on Sundays, but on all other six might properly be called a farmer.

HENRY FIELDING (1707–54)
of Parson Trulliber in *Joseph Andrews*

There is nothing like comparative religion for making one comparatively religious.

RONALD KNOX (1888–1957)

Religion is the opium of the people.

CHARLES KINGSLEY (1819–75)

The plain old religion of the Church of England, which is now almost everywhere spoken against, under the new name of Methodism.

JOHN WESLEY
15 October 1739
Journal

Preachers are born not made . . . Of course, sometimes they are born in later life.

ANON

God does not comfort us to make us comfortable, but to make us comforters.

JOHN HENRY JOWETT (1817–93)

Philosophers and clergyman are always discussing why we should be good, as if anyone doubted that he ought to be.

G.M. TREVELYAN (1876–1962)

An utterly lonely, poverty stricken minister in an utterly unresponsive village, with an ill wife and no servants, who rang his own bell daily, said his offices and made his meditation and never lost heart . . . is the true evidence of the supernatural.

EVELYN UNDERHILL (1875–1941)

What use are the phrases of the New Testament or Hymn book to me: So full of 'advancing the kingdom' and 'onward Christian soldiers?' Here are we at St. Luke's with a congregation of seven or eight every Sunday, where we used to be seventy or eighty. What we need most these days is a theology of decline.

GEORGE HAVARD
United Reformed Minister
1968

I preach forever, but I preach in vain.
GEORGE CRABBE (1754–1832)

There are no short cuts to heaven, only the ordinary way of ordinary things.
VINCENT MCNABB OP

It is so difficult to forgive God.
VINCENT MCNABB OP

Against her foes Religion well defends.
Her sacred truths, but often fears her friends.
GEORGE CRABBE (1754–1832)

Walked to call on old Rossiter and his wife . . . Read the prayers to him for the sick . . . During the time I was waiting downstairs, as the girl told me I could not go into her bedroom just then, I examined her in the Catechism, but found her very imperfect, and told her if she could say it by next Sunday, I would give her a shilling.
JOHN SKINNER
2 March 1827

The function of any Christian church is to help people to pray, to help them relate to God. The Church of England has always been a good place in which to pray, and it still is.
WILLIAM REES-MOGG
The Times, 14 October 1993

No praying, it spoils business.

THOMAS OTWAY

Lest O Lord this prayer be too obscure, permit thy servant to illustrate it with an anecdote.

METHODIST MINISTER
invited only to say the prayers, when he had fully expected to preach
quoted by Allan M. Laing, *Prayers and Graces* (1944)

A long unwieldy prayer, conceived on the sudden though not so suddenly uttered.

HENRY KING (1592–1669)
Bishop of Chichester

You are now a parson's wife, and must claim no precedence over any of your parishioners.

GEORGE HERBERT (1593–1633)
A Priest to the Temple

A clergyman has nothing to do but be slovenly and selfish – read the newspaper, watch the weather, and quarrel with his wife.

JANE AUSTEN (1775–1817)
Mansfield Park

There was another marriage this morning. Indeed the bride behaved so bad by laughing and other misconduct, I was obliged to say I would stop the ceremony; and the man who gave her away put on his hat in the midst of the Church. The clerk, White, asked whether they might ring. I said, Yes, a peal or two, as was customary at marriage; but not make the Church a drinking place, as they had done last Thursday.

JOHN SKINNER
22 January 1827

SEPTEM. 7. . . . Had three bottles of Wine out of my room in ye B.C.R. this afternoon and Waring had another, out of his room. Waring was very drunk and Bedford was but little better. N.B. I was very sober, as I had made a resolution never to get drunk again, when in Geree's rooms in April last, when I fell down dead, and cut my Occiput (back of the head) very bad indeed.

JAMES WOODFORDE
The Diary of a Country Parson
1763

It may be your five hundredth funeral. But it is their only one. It may be your third baptism that week, but they will never have another.

PREBENDARY KENNETH HAWORTH

I was half way through my first baptism, when a woman said 'hey guv. this lot isn't in our service sheets'. Nor was it. I had given them the order for Christian burial, by mistake.

DAVID PINK
Curate of St Michael's, Ilford, 1960

The Lord said to me, try to be as good as people think you are.

FRANCIS OF ASSISI (1181/2–1226)

The Church was well attended and I preached on the gospel . . . Called upon Sarah Somer at Red Hill, near the Poor House. She had an inflammation on the chest, and seems in great fear of dying. I made some strong exhortations, and told her I could give no hopes that a mere faith could save her, in case she were called from this world to another; she must sincerely repent of her past sins, which had been many and grievous to my knowledge. This woman has been as bad as anyone in the Parish, and has brought up all her family in the same licentious course; but now she is in a most frightful state. The end will be the Methodists will immediately get round her, and if she says she has firm faith, they will give her a viaticum, and make this worst of sinners, for the edification of the parish, die a saint.

JOHN SKINNER
4 February 1827

Christianity is a heroism.

BARON VON HÜGEL (1852–1925)

Christianity is a religion of motives.
FREDERICK W. FABER (1814–63)

There is no holy communion without holy community.
BISHOP JOHN ROBINSON

Pour out that you may be filled.
AUGUSTINE OF HIPPO (345–430)

As I take my shoes from the shoemaker and my coat from the tailor, so I take my religion from the priest.
SAMUEL JOHNSON (1709–84)

There is a vast difference between the despair of one who rejects God, and the desperation of the man that leads him to throw himself into the arms of God.
JOHN WARD
on the suicide of a fellow priest
funeral address 1994

Don't listen to the outside so much. Listen to the quiet within.
THOMAS À KEMPIS (*c.* 1380–1471)

Then, dear friends, it is sinful to postpone purposes of service. If you have some grand project and holy purpose, I would ask you not to delay it. My dear friend, Mr William Olney, was here, he was there, he was everywhere, serving his Lord and Master; and now that he is suddenly stricken down, his life cannot be said to be in any sense unfinished. There is nothing left undone with regard to anybody.

. . . Mr Whitfield said that he would not go to bed unless he had put even his gloves in the right place. If he should die in the night, he would not like to have anybody asking 'Where did he leave his gloves?' That is the way for a Christian man always to live; have everything in order, even to a pair of gloves.

C.H. SPURGEON (1834–92)
sermon at the Metropolitan Tabernacle, Newington, on Thursday evening, 16 October 1890

That monstrous black-coated race.

W.M. THACKERAY (1811–63)
The Book of Snobs

A clergyman is privileged to be a bit of a fool, you know: it's ony becoming in 'is profession.

GEORGE BERNARD SHAW (1856–1950)
Candida

There is not in the universe a more ridiculous, nor a more contemptible animal, than a proud clergyman.

HENRY FIELDING (1707–54)

'I always thought Graham would have made a good parson, only he doesn't believe in God.'
'That's no handicap these days,' Mr Turnbull said.

ALAN BENNETT (1934–)
Talking Heads

It may be that only men who have no intense, personal, passionate life of their own drift into the ministry, and again, it may be that the ministerial habit itself tends to foster such impersonality, to crush out all the intense, tearing impulses that make the essence of the lives of most of us.

GAMALIEL BRADFORD
Letters

I had the satisfaction of managing to walk from Hay to Clyro by the fields without meeting a single person, always a great triumph to me and a subject for warm self congratulation for I have a peculiar dislike to meeting people, and a peculiar liking for a deserted road.

FRANCIS KILVERT
7 April 1870

Some ministers would make good martyrs. They are so dry they would burn well.

C.H. SPURGEON (1834–92)

MAY 23. . . . was examined for deacon's Orders, and I came of very well. I was set over in the middle of the fifth Chapter of St. Paul to the Romans and construed that Chapter quite to the end. I was quite half an hour examining. He asked a good many hard and deep questions. I had not one question that Yes, or No, would answer . . . Mr Hewish is a very fair Examiner, and will see whether a Man be read or not soon.

JAMES WOODFORDE
The Diary of a Country Parson 1763

Lord, make me good but not yet.

AUGUSTINE OF HIPPO (354–430)

I prepared a sermon on the Gospel for the day. 'Except your righteousness exceed the righteousness of the Scribes and Pharisees.' There were very few at Church in the morning, as it rained hard.

JOHN SKINNER
18 July 1830

In the ministerial life it is not so much the doing of the duties; it is not so much the sort of sermon that is being preached as the sort of man that is behind the sermon.

J. PATERSON SMYTH

APRIL 30. . . . I got up this morning at two o'clock to get or make a sermon for Farmer Bertelet's funeral this afternoon, and by twelve o'clock I had finished almost all of it.

JAMES WOODFORDE
The Diary of a Country Parson 1764

The important thing about a sermon is not that it is remembered, but that it is received.

PREBENDARY KENNETH HAWORTH

But I would especially direct your attention to that word 'passionate'. We have most of us, I suppose, listened to Hitler on the wireless. I am not suggesting that we should preach like that. But I wish that we could all preach – and I know men who have done it – with as much earnestness, as much zeal, as much prophetic fervour, as though the Word of God, which we are feebly trying to utter in our sermons, were verily and indeed the most urgent and the most important thing in all the world: because, of course, it is.

CHARLES SMYTH
The Art of Preaching
1940

If gold rust, what shall iron do?
For if a priest be foul, on whom we trust
No wonder is a lewd man to rust.

GEOFFREY CHAUCER (*c.*1343–1400)
The Canterbury Tales

Monday May 10th.

I began visiting my parishioners in order, from house to house; for which I set apart the time when they cannot work, because of heat, viz. from twelve to three in the afternoon.

JOHN WESLEY (1703–91)
Journal

Blessed is that friar who loves his brother as much when he is sick and can be of no use to him as when he is well.

FRANCIS OF ASSISI (1181/2–1226)

While the Bible urges us all to love our neighbour, it says nothing about rival footballers, which is how it came to pass that a football match between a church and the Salvation Army turned into a battle that left five players injured. Mike McGill, 47, a Baptist minister, broke his ankle. Two players broke their noses. Two others were substituted after suffering shoulder and leg injuries. The good news is that this religious clash at Sheringham, Norfolk, is only an annual fixture. The disturbing news is that it is billed as a friendly match.

THE TIMES
11 January 1994

JULY 16. . . . For throwing some Wine last night in Bedford's face in the B.C.R. I was sconced a Bottle of Wine, which I pd. this evening to the B.C.R.

JAMES WOODFORDE
The Diary of a Country Parson
1763

If God spare my life, ere many years I will cause a boy that driveth the plough shall know more of the scripture than thou doest.

WILLIAM TYNDALE (?1494–1536)

At first the bishop counselled but one step, recommended but one remedy, had but one medicine . . . he prescribed the archdeacon.

ANTHONY TROLLOPE (1815–82)
The Warden

The Church of England is certainly a tolerant church. It tolerates the utterly intolerable!

ANON

Yes, I remember my confirmation. The vicar came over to see my father and said, isn't it about time Harry was confirmed. When my father agreed the vicar told him, the thing to remember is, do not let him have Brylcreem on his hair. It gets on the bishop's hands! This proved the entire content of my preparation.

CANON H.C.F. COPSEY
Vicar of East Grinstead, 1967

The growing good of the world is partly dependent on unhistoric acts; and that things are not so ill with you and me as they might have been, is half owing to the number who lived faithfully a hidden life, and rest in unvisited tombs.

GEORGE ELIOT (1819–80)
Middlemarch
on the life of Dorothea, the clergyman's wife

Every man desires to live long, but no man would be old.
DEAN JONATHAN SWIFT (1667–1745)

Before a man comes to be wise, he is half dead with gouts and consumption.
BISHOP JEREMY TAYLOR (1613–67)

Can an Archdeacon be saved?
MEDIEVAL SCHOLASTIC QUESTION

All that we really know about Hell, is that it is a state that exists because God has told us so. We are not bound to believe there is anyone in it.
BRUCE MARSHALL

And when you're down in the fiery pit, weeping and gnashing your teeth it will be no good looking up to Heaven and pleading 'Lord, we didna ken, we didna ken.' God will look down from his heavenly throne and reply: 'Well, ye ken noo.'
SCOTTISH MINISTER ON THE ISLAND OF LEWIS

I dreamt last night I was in purgatory. I thought to myself, the Roman Catholics were right after all.
CANON A.L. LILLEY
to his daughter Geraldine

What they do in heaven we are ignorant of, of what they do not do we are told expressly, that they neither marry, nor are given in marriage.

DEAN JONATHAN SWIFT (1667–1745)

Write with speed now for I cannot tell how long I may last.

THE VENERABLE BEDE (673–735)

You will sleep well if your heart doesn't blame you.

THOMAS À KEMPIS (*c*.1380–1471)

Having learnt that Charles Dando of Cridlingcot was killed by a fall from is horse whilst riding from Bristol, I walked to his house to enquire after his family. My anxiety on their account was soon relieved, as I found them sitting round a large table, regaling themselves, without any apparent emotion.

JOHN SKINNER
1821

Life is not measured by the time we live.

GEORGE CRABBE (1754–1832)

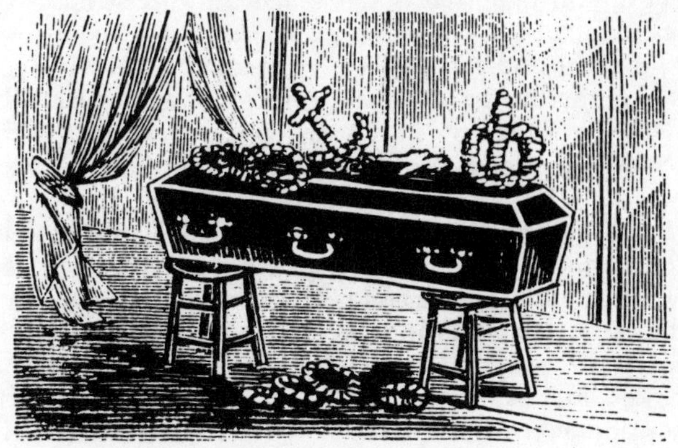

The coffin seemed very heavy. As the procession moved across College Green to the Cloister arch, the men staggered under the weight and the coffin lurched and tilted to one side over the short bearer. One very fat man had constituted himself chiefest mourner of all and walked next to the coffin before my father and myself . . .

So the clergy and choir came to meet us at the door, then turned up the Cathedral nave chanting in solemn procession, 'I am the Resurrection and the Life saith the Lord'. But meanwhile there was a dreadful struggle at the steps leading up from the Cloisters to the door. The bearers were quite unequal to the task and the coffin seemed crushingly heavy. There was a stamping and a scuffling, a mass of struggling men swaying to and fro, pushing and writhing and wrestling while the coffin sank and rose and sank again. Once or twice I thought the whole mass of men must have been down together with the coffin atop of them and some one killed or maimed at least. But now came the time of the fat chief mourner.

Seizing his opportunity he rushed into the strife by an opening large and the rescued coffin rose. At last by a wild effort and tremendous heave the ponderous coffin was borne up the steps and through the door into the Cathedral where the choristers, quite unconscious of the scene and the fearful struggle going on behind, were singing up the nave like a company of angels.

In the Choir there was another dreadful struggle to let the coffin down. The bearers were completely overweighted, they bowed and bent and nearly fell and threw the coffin down on the floor. When it was safely deposited we all retired to seats right and left and a verger or beadle, in a black gown and holding a mace, took up his position at the head of the coffin, standing. The Psalm was sung nicely to a very beautiful chant. The Dean had gout and could not appear.

FRANCIS KILVERT (1840–79)
at Worcester Cathedral
Friday 2 December 1870

I breakfasted with Temple and then went to the Temple Church and heard a very good sermon on 'Set thy house in order, for thou shalt shortly die.' This with the music and the good building put me into a very devout frame, and after service my mind was left in a pleasing calm state.

JAMES BOSWELL
London Journal
10 April 1763

All have won and all shall have the prizes.

LEWIS CARROLL
(Revd C. L. Dodgson, 1832–98)

Tho' with great difficulty I am got hither, yet now I do not repent me of all the trouble I have been at to arrive where I am.

JOHN BUNYAN (1626–88)
The Pilgrim's Progress

October 17, Sunday . . . Very weak this morning, scarce able to put on my cloaths and with great difficulty, get downstairs with help. Mr. Dade read Prayers & Preached this morning at Weston Church – Nancy at church. Mr. & Mrs. Custance & Lady Bacon at church. Dinner today, rost beef etc.

JAMES WOODFORDE
The Diary of a Country Parson
last entry in his diary, 1802

Faith is a lively thing, mighty in working, valient and strong, ever doing, ever fruitful . . . He asketh not whether good works are to be done or not, but has done them already, ere mention be made of them; and is always doing for such is his nature.

WILLIAM TYNDALE (?1494–1536)

Pray for me as I do for you, that we may merrily meet in heaven.

THOMAS MORE (1478–1535)

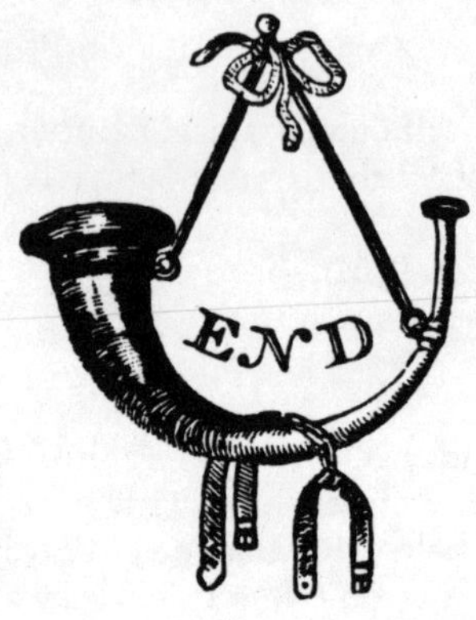
END